SAN DIEGO POETRY ANNUAL 2025

San Diego Entertainment + Arts Guild

San Diego, California

San Diego Entertainment and Arts Guild (SDEAG)
1953 Huffstatler St., Suite A
Rainbow, CA 92028
760 458-2704 (text)
760 728-2088 (message)

sandiegopoetryannual.com
sdpoetryannual@gmail.com
@sdpoetryannual

sdeag.org
sdeag1@gmail.com

© San Diego Entertainment and Arts Guild (SDEAG)
    All rights reserved

No part of this book may be reproduced, stored in a retrieval system or transmitted by any means without the express written consent of the Publisher.

First published by San Diego Entertainment and Arts Guild on March 1, 2026.

ISBN: 9798244155839

Printed in the United States of America.

The views expressed in this collection of poems are solely those of the poet and do not necessarily reflect the views of the Publisher, and the Publisher hereby disclaims any responsibility for them.

Contents

Logan Hanek
  Ode to the Cheeseburgers — 2
Roz McCarty
  Ode to Boba — 3
Elana Rose Hebert
  I have a million dogs — 4
Tripp Marino
  Ode to My Dog — 5
Meadow Smith
  Gobble! Gobble! Gobble! — 6
Ana Carolina Ortiz
  Ode to My Dog — 7
Korbin Cruz
  I am Bulbasaur — 8
Julius Hernandez
  Ode to My Brother — 9
Lindsey Adams
  Hot Cheetos — 10
Zachary Winters
  Ode to My Mom and Dad — 11
Liam Hoffman
  Tung Sahur — 12
Gabriella Mayorquin
  Oh My Cat — 13
Hailey Gorney
  I Am a Tree — 14
Kayla Castro
  Ode to My Parents — 15
Dawson Poppert
  Ode to My Dogs — 16
Braedan O'Neal
  Roses Are Red — 17
Liam Shanahan
  Ode to My Beautiful Rat — 18
Donovan Brittain
  Twinkle, Twinkle — 19
Charlotte Mata
  Ode to My Mom — 20
Lukas Perez
  Maybe cats can't fly like bats — 21
Isaiah Chatman
  Odes — 22
Daanish Kohistani
  I Dribble My Soccer Ball — 23

Oliver White
- **Ode to My Cat** — 24

Capri Lampard
- **Playing** — 25

Henley James Gordon
- **Ode to The USA** — 26

Savannah Chatman
- **Roses are red, violets are blue** — 27

Joshua Singer
- **Ode to My Dog** — 28

Rayland Hinkel
- **Heavy Metal** — 29

Lionel Ceja Murua
- **Ode to My Japan** — 30

Ellie Douglas
- **1, 2, 3!** — 31

Koa Morris
- **Ode to My Mom** — 32

Adison Johnson
- **Roses are red** — 33

Ellie Burns
- **Ode to My Dog** — 34

Jade Gagliardi
- **I Am So Still** — 35

Rose Lieder
- **An Ode to My Friends** — 36

Camden Adam,
- **I Am Scary** — 37

Wyatt Lee
- **Ode to Dinosaurs** — 38

P.K. Iverson
- **I have billions of dogs** — 39

Alena Gagliardi
- **Ode to Mrs. Miller** — 40

Reagan Cruz
- **I Hate Halloween** — 41

Lucy Erlandson
- **Ode to Country Music** — 42

Zachariah Hutson
- **I'm hairy—Godzilla** — 43

Maverick Cooper
- **Ode to My Dog** — 44

Remi Duarte
- **I'm short** — 45

McKenna Usry
    Ode to My Cat   46
Phoenix Cady
    I Am as Tall as a Giraffe   47
Genevieve Gagliardi
    Ode to My Cat   48
Harper Cartwright
    Hair   49
Jane Hoagland
    Ode to My Bunnies   50
Scarlett George
    My Name is Scar   51
Dovie Brittain
    Ode to My Cat   52
Hunter Sparks
    I am so heavy   53
Isla Harbison
    Ode to My Headphones   54
Axel Martin
    School is Boring   55
Aubrey Phillips
    Oh, Candy   56
Ryder Dawson
    There's a Flower   57
Charley Shy
    Soccer   58
Izzie Douglas
    I have red hair   59
Myles Decker
    Oh, Cheetah   60
Dustin Clark
    I Love The Grinch   61
Tyler Michels
    Oh, Nature   62
Aurora McNatt
    My name is Justin   63
Layla Shelesh
    Soccer   64
Bodhi Kern
    I Am 32 Years Old   65
Nessa Taft
    Oh, Wendy's   66
Kaylee Smith
    My name is Lilah   67

Clementine Harris-Young
    Oh, books!   68
Juniper Keeble
    I have 1,000 puppies   69
Ashton Martin
    Ode to My Sister   70
Sayuri Levesque
    I Have Red Hair   71
Brayden Windle
    Oh, wolverines   72
Hector Ortiz
    My Dad Is Mr. Beast   73
Solveig Hodson
    Merry Christmas   74
Sawyer Yohe
    I have gold hair   75
    I Am Bald   75
Zoe Taylor
    Red Panda   76
Lilah Lee
    My Name Is Cow   77
Maddy Peterson
    Ode to My Dog, Mo   78
River Thorton
    Time   79
Aaron Ruvalcaba
    Roxy and Ellie   80
Brody Kai Alberti
    I Am 70 Years Old   81
Sofia Perez
    Oh, My Dog   82
Zeke Harbinson
    Some Lies   83
Alice Reyes
    The Hardest Workers   84
Trenton Catlin
    Hello, Bacon Hair   85
J.R. Burns
    Ode to My Best Friend   86
Cyrus Hernandez
    Ode to Gorillas   87
Riley Farlow
    Watch Me   88
Brynn Shaw
    Ode to Jellybeans   89

Sarah Ceja
    Swing   90
Ella Marjanovich
    Ode to My Sticker Chart   91
Leo Christobal
    The Soccer Ball   92
Sadie Ann Fransway
    Ode to My Loved Ones   93
Blake Zietlow
    I can tell you the time   94
Anders Schumaier
    Ode to My Beautiful Dog   95
Lorelai Dewey
    The Amazing Cup   96
    Dancing Snowflakes   96
    Can you guess what I am?   96
Emily Ornelas
    Ode to Shelter Pups   97
Miranda Ortiz
    Cats   98

DRAWINGS

    Braceah Ohiai   99
    Joel Scarlett   99
    Avey May   100
    Nolan Hunter   100
    Mason Slade   101
    Robert Yohe IV   101

THANKS   102

ACKNOWLEDGMENTS   102

CREDITS   102

KIDS!
SAN DIEGO POETRY ANNUAL
2025

YING WU
Executive Editor

AMEERAH HOLLIDAY
Editor

Founding Editor
RAE ROSE

Logan Hanek

Ode to the Cheeseburgers

The soft bread and crunchy lettuce,
the crispy, salty, delicious galore of the patty.
The balanced favor. Refreshingly
rich with the mayonnaise, mustard,
and ketchup all together.
Ode to all in one of soft, crunchy,
crispy, salty, delicious,
refreshing rich flavor of my dad's juicy burger.

Roz McCarty

Ode to Boba

To all the bobas!
Pink! Blue!
Bobas are always the best,
no matter what.
You're my favorite drink
no matter what.

Elana Rose Hebert

I have a million dogs

and I am a very short girl.
The smallest.
I turn my sister into stone,
and my dog—all my dogs—
are so big. I live at New York.
My feet smell like dirty socks.

Tripp Marino

Ode to My Dog

You are fluffy and golden.
Your chest is fluffy
like golden clouds.
Your jaws are so strong
you carry logs
in through the doggy door.
You are the best
dog I could have asked for.

Meadow Smith

Gobble! Gobble! Gobble!

I'm a turkey, soaring through the wind,
trying to escape those who want to EAT ME!
Yes, yes, yes, it's Thanksgiving
in less than two weeks.
Will I survive another year?
I hope so. Someone, something
will rise upon me,
save Turkey Island.
I should survive another year—
until next Thanksgiving.

       T   Thanksgiving
       U   Unity
       R   Recipes
       K   Kitchen
       E   Exciting
       Y   Yum

Ana Carolina Ortiz

Ode to My Dog

You are my favorite puppy in the world.
I love being with you.
You are so cute and pretty,
like the sunshine.
I love you
because you
are fluffy and always
play with me at the beach.
You are as colorful
as the sand from the sea.

Korbin Cruz

I am Bulbasaur

When I woke up
the sun
gave me a warm hug.
The flowers on my back,
ready for the new day.
I am now an Ivysaur.

Julius Hernandez

Ode to My Brother

What's funny is, I am rude
when I wake up my brother.
He is fast asleep in the morning.
My brother, who is my best friend,
with his yellow, funny hair.
Ode to my brother,
you make my life so rare.

Lindsey Adams

Hot Cheetos

Oh, hot Cheetos!
Spicy, hot, red.
Spicy—but sweet,
I could eat the spicy
red glaze.
You set my heart
ablaze.

Zachary Winters

Ode to My Mom and Dad

Dad, you are hard-working.
You are the one who puts
a roof over our heads,
who puts food on our plates.
You are the one who helps me
with important stuff at school.
Mom, you are the one who helps
me with reading.
You are the one who helps me read
and keep going with baseball.
I love you, Mom and Dad.

Liam Hoffman

Tung Sahur

Tung tung sahur
swung his bat
to and fro
with the wind
tung sahur go
real slow
brr brr
pata pim flow
and slow
cooler than ice
nowhere to go

Gabriella Mayorquin

Oh My Cat!

You're fluffy as a feather.
You remind me of a cheetah.
You have beautiful green
eyes like leaves.
With dark brown fur,
you are my best friend.
Thank you for always
being on my side.
When I'm sad,
you smell like hibiscus flowers.

Hailey Gorney

I Am a Tree

I can move my leaves.
People climb on me
and jump off.
I was right.
I should have been a plant.

Kayla Castro

Ode to My Parents

Oh, my lovely parents.
The percentage of my love
and respect for you is higher
than the white fluffy clouds in the sky.
I am as thankful as much as I am water
and life and earth. Your smile is the light to my life.
Without you, I would be dull as a pencil
that hadn't been sharpened in five years.

Dawson Poppert
Ode to My Dogs

You are so nice. Your brown fur looks like oak wood.
You are as beautiful as a rose garden.
Your eyes are as green as a lime.

Braedan O'Neal

Roses are red

Roses are red,
violets are blue—
I can't believe
I fell for you.

Liam Shanahan

Ode to My Beautiful Rat

You are as fluffy as snow.
When you cuddle me,
you smell like pumpkin pie.
You are as black
as the night sky.

Donovan Brittain

Twinkle, twinkle,
like a star,
I would push you off a plane so high —
laugh when you fall from the sky.

Charlotte Mata

Ode to My Mom

I love your curly brown hair,
brown like chocolate.
I love when you make me breakfast
on the weekends.
Hot, crunchy bacon
and soft sweet pancakes.
I love your warm hugs.
I feel so safe and cozy.

Lukas Perez

Maybe cats can't fly like bats.
They just need a kick,
so they don't have a tick.
Now they can fly,
so they can eat a fly.

Isaiah Chatman

Odes

To my sweet, loved dog—
you make me feel like a person
who never feels out of reach,
with your fluffy fur that you always snuggle with me.

To my friends—
you are always there for me.
You make me feel like
I do not deserve you
from how nice you are.

Daanish Kohistani

I Dribble My Soccer Ball

dodging my opponents
like a gazelle, like a cheetah!
Zig, zag, zoom!
To the goal I go!

Oliver White

Ode to My Cat

You are as sweet as candy,
fluffy like a cloud.
You love when I pet you.
Oh, my sweet cat!
When you see me
come through the door
you stomp over with your
fluffy gray fur. Oh, my cat!
On my saddest days,
you remove my sadness.

Capri Lampard

Playing

with my little brother is
like a racecar.
He is fast
as lightning.

Henley James Gordon

Ode to the USA

Oh, *Star Spangled Banner,*
your flag is flying higher
than any God that was created.
Your country is more beautiful
than thousands of waving oceans.
Your country is more free
than a dog without a cage.

Savannah Chatman

Roses are red, violets are blue
I love my family,
so you should, too.

Joshua Singer

Ode to My Dog

I love you. You jump
on top of me and lick me
and lie down with me when I go to sleep.
You are black and brown, and you have white
fur on your throat like snow.
I love you, Sasha.

Rayland Hinkel

Heavy Metal

Heavy metal, you
are a way to let out anger.
Heavy metal,
you are the best genre
of music.

Lionel Ceja Murua

Ode to My Japan

Your cherry blossoms bloom in spring
like a rising sun. Ode to my Japan.
Your people have millions of ideas to create things in the
　　universe.
Ode to my Japan—your mountains shine like the moon.

Ellie Douglas

1, 2, 3!

Get ready to cheer!
Hear me say
watch me all day.
We start and jump,
see what happens next —
we do it great!
It might seem hard to do it right
but try very hard
and you'll do alright.

Koa Morris

Ode to My Mom

My beautiful mom!
I love your
brown soft hair.
Your voice
is as pretty
as a flower.
Your smile is as bright
as a sun. Your kind
personality reminds me
of an angel.

Adison Johnson

Roses are red

violets are blue.
Softball is better,
and I should know, too.

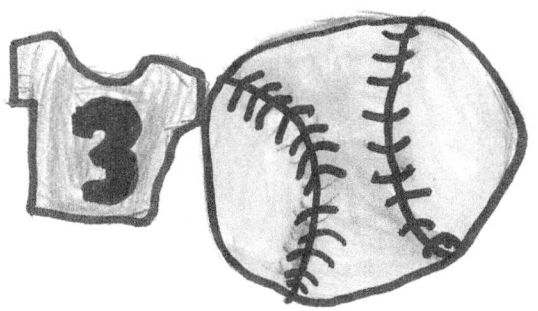

Ellie Burns

Ode to My Dog

Oh my dog, I love it when you wag
your tail at me. You are as a brown
as a tree trunk, and as gold
as your future. You light me up
with happiness. You bite,
but you protect.
You smell like flowers
after you get groomed
and feel as fluffy
as a carpet. Oh!
I love you, Chicharron.

Jade Gagliardi

I Am So Still

I live in the sun.
It is so peaceful.
When I feel the kids
come out and play
it is so peaceful.
When the kids all leave
and then sun starts to set,
I fall asleep
and it is so peaceful.

Rose Lieder

An Ode to My Friends

Oh, friends! You make me
feel like I don't deserve you.
You are always there for me
and you support me.
Whenever I need you
you come in a flash.
You're my peanut butter to my jam
and I wish you know now
how much you matter.
I will always be there for you, too!
Thank you.

Camden Adam

I Am Scary

and hairy.
I am one billion years old.
I am tinier than an ant
and bigger than a blue whale.
I am older than dinosaurs.
I can lift the moon.
I throw the sun onto the ground.

My name is Dust.
I live in a tree.
I eat all of us.

Wyatt Lee

Ode to Dinosaurs

The walking prehistoric lizards
we know so much, also so little.
Your cousins are in the sky.
Ode to how much I love you,
but all we have are fossils.
We are trying to bring you back
and hopefully we do.
I love your mystery and I wonder—
what did you sound like?
What was your color?
What did you actually look like?
We have some theories
and evidence in your bones.
How much I love you.
How much I wish to see you.

P.K. Iverson

I have billions of dogs

and every toy
and a hundred sisters.
I am 11,000 years old
and I ride on a tiger.
I could fly to school,
but I don't do it.

Alena Gagliardi

Ode to Mrs. Miller

with your nice smiles
and your kindness.
Oh, Mrs. Miller!
How you always help me,
your smile that is as bright as the sun!
You are as kind as a teacher can get.
You help me when I'm sad,
you help me when I need it.
Thank you for everything you do.

Reagan Cruz

I Hate Halloween

I Hate Halloween
I have a million dogs.
I have very short hair.
I hate pumpkins.
I don't go to the rodeo on the weekends.
Dogs are the worst pet ever.
Spiders are the best pet ever.
I hate cake.

Lucy Erlandson

Ode to Country Music

This is the way I want to sing.
My heart relies on the soft tunes.
Dolly Parton. There is nothing
like a Luke Comb song while at the river,
a Morgan Waller song at the desert.
My love for you is unforgettable.
I love a Megan Moroney song in the car.
This is my love letter to country music.

Zachariah Hutson

I'm hairy—Godzilla

I have a green bird and nine dogs.
My dog is black and his name is Hatzi.
My arch nemesis is Zeke.

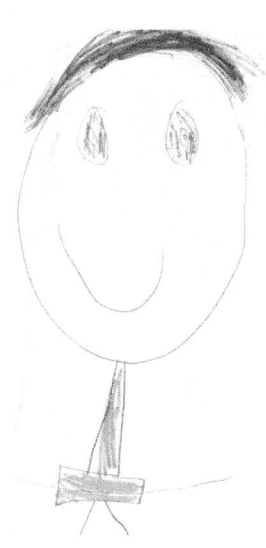

Maverick Cooper

Ode to My Dog

You are so cute!
So cute like a mouse.
You are so big like a mountain.
Your colors are so dark like the night
and bright like the sun.
You make me feel so good.

Remi Duarte

I'm short

I live in Japan.
I'm gigantic.
I have blue eyes.
I have purple hair.
I destroy everything,
I'm a jet.
I fly 1,000 miles per hour.
My motor breaks,
sometimes I crash land.
I go so fast I break the sound barrier.

McKenna Usry

Ode to My Cat

You come to bed for me at night.
Cuddle me from dusk 'til dawn.
How much I love you!
You're my little cuddle buddy
and you make me feel so safe
when you're in my arms at night.

Phoenix Cady

I Am as Tall as a Giraffe

I have lots of exotic fish.
I'm a monkey.
I have a pumpkin face.
I'm an animal.
I live in the bottom of the ocean.
I have a pet piranha.
I have eyes that stick out very long.
I'm from a new planet.
I live with trilobites.

Genevieve Gagliardi

Ode to My Cat

My wonderful cat, May!
Amazing personality!
Fills my heart with joy!
Two years old,
you're a playful girl.
You snuggle me every night.
Ode to May.

Harper Cartwright

Hair

My name is Lilah.
I have red hair.
I have a sister and a brother.
I can shape shift
and I am 20 years old,
but I look like I am 5 years old,
I live with my cousin
and my cousin lives with them, too.
My mom has blue hair,
my dad has golden hair,
and my brother has green hair.
My grandma has rainbow hair
and my grandpa has grey hair.
My cousin has pink hair.

Jane Hoagland

Ode to My Bunnies

Soft as clouds,
your brown spots
are as brown as a tree.
Your whiteness
is like snow on the street.
Little snowball tails.
Oh! I love you
Pumpkin and Spice
for being here with me.

Scarlett George

My name is Scar

I live in Mexico.
I'm afraid of clowns.
I'm the king of the school.
I'm 80 years old.
I can walk on the roof.
I have a pet named Piggy.
My mom's name is Rose.
I have a friend named Piggy.

Dovie Brittain

Ode to My Cat

Dear Bubbas,
you are adorable, you are fluffy!
You are black with white stripes!
Whenever I am sad
you always cheer me up
I hope you are always by my side.

Hunter Sparks

I Am So Heavy

I am so heavy,
like a rock.

Isla Harbison

Ode to My Headphones

Oh, my wonderful headphones!
Thank you very much
for keeping my ears warm
when it is cold out.
Thank you for letting me listen to music
and thank you for letting me draw on you.

    Sincerely,
        Isla Harbison

Axel Martin

School is Boring

At school
there are no things
to do
except lunch,
except recess.
Checklists
are so long,
it felt like a year
just to read it.
Lunch
and recess.

Aubrey Phillips

Oh, Candy

Oh, candy,
you are so yummy—
what would I do without you?
Oh, candy, you give
me energy
but just not enough.
Oh, candy,
I want to eat you
all day long,
but no. No.
I will not.
Oh, candy, you give me joy,
but you are not good for me.
Oh, candy,
you are not healthy for me,
and you will never be.
Oh, Candy,
you will not be with me
forever —
so goodbye, candy,
goodbye.

Ryder Dawson

There's a Flower

on the counter.
Outside,
in the breeze,
it shakes.

Charley Shy

Soccer

Oh, soccer, how wonderful you are!
You helped me uncover what I want to do.
I love playing and having fun.
In soccer, you have to run.
A soccer ball is round,
so I love what I have found.
Every Saturday
there is a game. I hope
it stays the same.
I hope I get better with my friend,
and keep playing until the end.
I'm on a team with my best friend
and I hope it stays like that.
Right now I like where I'm at.
In soccer, there is a blocker.
Soccer is hard, you do not
want a red card.
Soccer is the best sport
in the whole world.

Izzie Douglas

I have red hair

I have red hair.
I am bad at reading.
I do not like Halloween.
I am very tall.
I do not like pumpkins.
I do not like playing.
I have a chocolate lab.
I like when it is windy.
I am not nice.
I am bad at writing.
I don't like treats.
I don't like fun.

Myles Decker

Oh, Cheetah

Oh cheetah, you are fast.
So am I.
You are cool.
You are yellow with black spots—
my favorite color and my favorite
animal. Oh, cheetah, you are awesome.

Dustin Clark

I Love The Grinch

My sister is the coolest.
I love to write.
I don't like Christmas.

Tyler Michels

Oh, Nature

You, with your beautiful green leaves,
bring my body to ease.
When the wind whispers
through the trees,
it brings me so much glee.
I plant the seed in the ground,
colorful flowers pop out of the ground.
As the birds chirp,
the wind whispers through
the over grown, green forest.

Aurora McNatt

My name is Justin

but I am really small
and I'm 10 years old.
My mom is Alex and my mom
is Steve. I have really long
red hair, black hair, white hair,
and I have nine thousand cousins.
I also have a twin
and I am allergic to cheese.
I have three sisters and zero brothers
and I am the littlest.

Layla Shelesh

Soccer

Oh, soccer, a wonderful sport.
Thank you for being here
for me to play. You are so fun
and the ball is black and white.
Thank you for helping me grow.
You run so much in soccer
and so I love soccer, and so should you!
I hope you stay the same and never change,
I hope I get better.
I play with my friend, I hope I always do.
I would keep playing soccer
'til the end. I love soccer and I'll never quit.
I hope I keep growing
and never stop. Soccer is hard
and on the path to being good
you can be blocked on the way.
That is end of my story now.
The end.

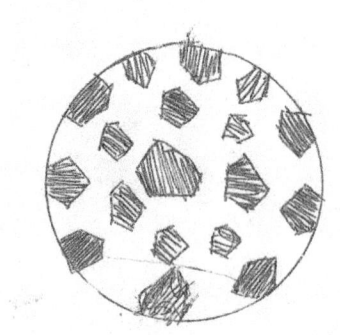

Bodhi Kern

I Am 32 Years Old

I have a best friend—
he has red hair
and I'm mad at my pants.
I go to a sad school.
My cat is a hot dog.
My boyfriend is flat.
I live in the North Pole
with a creepy home.
My friend and I live in a trash can
and hate books.

Nessa Taft

Oh, Wendy's

Oh, Wendy's, you bring
me joy and happiness.
So does the chili with the extra
cheese and the fries on the side.
Let's not forget about the cheeseburger,
and a small frosty
as well as a salad, fresh cookies
and chicken nuggets.
Now I am getting hungry.
Writing this. . .
should you sell this for free?

Kaylee Smith

My name is Lilah

I have a pumpkin friend.
Its name is Sophia.
I can see ghosts.
My friends are ghosts.
I also have skeleton friends.
My hair is purple.
My favorite school is Crest Spooky School.
And I love pumpkins.
It is a spooky school.

Clementine Harris-Young

Oh, books!

I flip through your pages
and read your words.
I look at your stories in my head.
Fiction or nonfiction,
I like them both.

Juniper Keeble

I have 1,000 puppies.
My dad is Justin Bieber.
My mom is Taylor Swift.
I am 13 years old.
My dad is 1,000 years old.
My mom is 3,
My sister is 1.

Ashton Martin

Ode to My Sister

Oh, my sister,
your eyes are like stars.
You love to dance.
My love for you will last
forever. You always
cheer me up.
Thank you for being my sister.

Sayuri Levesque

I Have Red Hair

and a pet tiger
and have 1,000 dogs
and I have a sister
who is an old cat.

Brayden Windle

Oh, wolverines

Not that many people know about you.
Your claws so sharp you could
cut through wood.
Your brown and black fur
protect you from the snow.
You're strong enough
to take down a Grisly Bear
or a Black Bear.

Hector Ortiz

My Dad Is Mr. Beast
My mom is a famous tennis player.
My brother owns a mansion, and I live with him.
My sister owns millions of kitties.

Solveig Hodson

Merry Christmas

Oh, Christmas,
thank you for the joy you bring.
From you to me, everything.
On your day I feel loved,
for that is the day we read
the stories of the angels above.
I love you dear, you holy day,
for you are the day
I say, "Hooray!"

Sawyer Yohe

I have gold hair,
my dad is Tom Brown,
my mom is Taylor Swift,
my teacher is my arch nemesis.
I live in Hawaii.
I am a soccer player.
My friend is Jason.

I am 100 years old.
I am weak.
I have 1,000 sisters
and 1,000 dollars.
I have a pool.

I am a YouTuber.

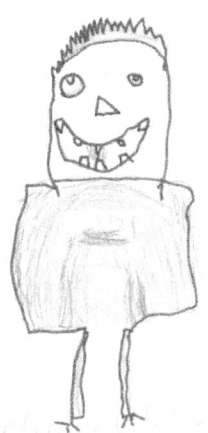

I am bald.
I am 100.
I have a farm.
I have rainbow dragons.
I have 10 siblings.
I am married to a capybara.
I live in a cave.
I have 1,000 toes.
My mom is Taylor Swift.
My dad is The Rock.
I have a 100 ladybugs.
I hate reading.
My birthday is on Christmas.
I love monsters.

Zoe Taylor

Red Panda

Oh, red panda. So cute and fluffy.
I love you so much,
from the bottom of my heart.
You eat bamboo
but you eat different things, too.
You are every single emotion.
You keep feeling through the day
and are adorable.
Red panda, you are adorable.
I love you.

Lilah Lee

My name is Cow

I am 80 years old.
I can walk on the ceiling.
My mom is a chicken.
My pet is a cloud,
I got a curse—
they made me look 7 years old.
I can draw very realistic.
My nemesis is Godzilla.
I love fish when it's raw.

Maddy Peterson

Ode to My Dog, Mo

You are fluffy, warm, and super cute.
Whenever I am sad,
you cheer me up.
You make me smile every day.
When I come back from school
you immediately run to greet me.
I love my dog, Mo.

River Thorton

Time

Inside a broken clock,
a man who will not die.
He will ring.
he will mock you.
It is time to go.

Aaron Ruvalcaba

Roxy and Ellie

to: Roxy and Ellie.
from: Aaron

Oh, my dogs —
you guys are so soft,
cute, fluffy, warm, kind.
You guys are playful
when I come home.
I love you Roxy and Ellie.

Brody Kai Alberti

I am 70 years old

I am the king of the school.
Bodhi and Elana are chasing me!!!
King Kong
and Godzilla
are here!
Shadow, Sonic, Silver. . .
Bodhi and Elana
are big and giant!!!

Here they are!

Sofia Perez

Oh, My Dog

Oh, my dog, you are black,
soft, pretty, warm and fluffy.
You speak your own language.
You are a good emotional support.
You bring everybody joy.

Zeke Harbinson

Some Lies

Pumkin spice tastes
like old lemonade.
I never work out.
My name is Ogooga.
My brother's name is Marshall.
The time is always 7:11.
On weekends,
I don't act like an animal.
Old men's toes taste like cake.

Alice Reyes

The Hardest Workers

Oh, my mom.
Oh, my dad.
Maybe the hardest workers of all time.
From the morning to the night,
you go to work as the sun wakes up
and falls right back.
One gives us food to eat
and one keeps the house shiny and bright.
One works until dark but is never gloomy.
Both give me hugs.
Dear mom and dad, I love you.

Trenton Catlin

Hello, Bacon Hair

You are cool, nice,
non-toxic, and supportive.
You are a good Roblox avatar.

J.R. Burns

Ode to My Best Friend

Oh, my best friend,
you make my day
brighter than I thought.
You are nice,
your smile soars
high as a kite.
You're my friend
to the end.

Cyrus Hernandez

Ode To Gorillas

Dear gorillas, you are big
and strong
and you're one of the biggest
types of monkeys.
Also, you can climb
the trees so good.

Riley Farlow

Watch Me

I am a fish.
Watch me spread.
If I am eaten—
I don't dread.

Brynn Shaw

Ode to Jellybeans

Oh, jellybeans,
you make my day bright.
Yes, some of you
are sweet or sour,
or a flavor no one likes.
You can be bitter or sweet.
So sweet!
Bad or good!
Oh, jellybean,
oh jellybean,
oh jellybean!
I will love you forever,
my jellybeans.

Sarah Ceja

Swing

I am a swing
swinging in the air.
I feel like a feather flying away.
I swing back and forth
like I am going to the sky,
like I would not come down.

Ella Marjanovich

Ode to My Sticker Chart

Oh, sticker chart,
my lovely sticker chart,
I love all of your colorful stickers.
Oh, my lovely sticker chart.

Leo Christobal

The Soccer Ball

The soccer ball glided across the grass
like a bird in the sky

Sadie Ann Fransway

Ode to My Loved Ones

Ode to my Mom, for love and care—
you can make me happy anywhere.
Ode to my Gramma
you help me grow
and not only that, but you help us know.
Ode to my dad
you take me on cool adventures,
you tease me the most,
but you're insane, and I love
that you venture.

Blake Zietlow

I can tell you the time.
I *click* and *clock* and *tic* and *toc*.
I am found in classrooms.
I can tell you the time.
I am a clock!

Anders Schumaier

Ode to My Beautiful Dog

I love you! You are so cute!
You are so nice to me!
You are very fluffy!
Your fur is like a night sky
and your name is Midnight.

Lorelai Dewey

The Amazing Cup

I am a cup, I drown every day.
I'm still alive when you
fill me up with drinks.
You can fill me up with drinks—
more than five.

Dancing Snowflakes

I am a snowflake,
dancing in the sky.
I fall and fall
down from the clouds.
Oh! I usually come
from the storms so loud.

Can you guess what I am?

I can help you with math,
I make anything. Oh, yes, I can!
I can make a star or
even make a rainbow car.
I make unicorns and dragons
and houses galore.
I am not a liquid, but I started from one.
I come in any color you want.
I am what candles are made of
and I will melt easily
Did you guess what I am?
Did you think I was a crayon?
Because I am!

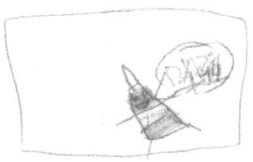

Emily Ornelas

Ode to Shelter Pups

I love the way you play on a rainy day.
I'd love to adopt you because you
would make me feel very lucky.
You're as soft as my teddy bear.
As I watch you, my little shelter pup,
you grow up. Your heart is very kind
and so is mine.
Will you be at my side?

Miranda Ortiz

Cats

are shivering in the rain,
hissing in pain.

Braceah Ohiai

Joel Scarlett

Avey May

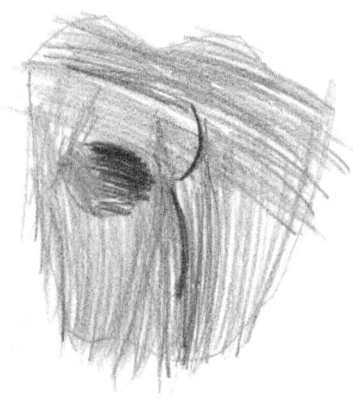

Nolan Hunter

Mason Slade

Robert Yohe IV

THANKS

to teachers at Crest School:
Mrs. Alegria, Ms. Olin, Mrs. Podwoski, and **Mrs. Miller**

to Crest School Principal: **Michael Kuhfal**

to **Kelsey Smith** for assisting with the workshops

ACKNOWLEDGMENTS

Crest School in Crest (El Cajon) allowed poet-teacher **Rae Rose** to conduct four workshops that produced the poems and drawings included in the *KSDPA 2025*.

The *KSDPA* and its sponsoring non-profit, San Diego Entertainment and Arts Guild, are grateful to the students and staff for participating in this celebration of poetry and The Arts.

CREDITS

Front cover: *Girl with Hearts*
  Josephine Denesowicz

  Dancing girl (inset at title)
  Elana Rose Hebert

Frontispiece: *Family*
  Alice Reyes

Back cover:
  (left to right, in rows—top to bottom)

Mason Slade, Adison Johnson, Zoe Taylor;

Miles Decker, Jade Gagliardi, Sarah Ceja;

Riley Farlow;

Clementine Harris-Young, Aaron Ruvalcaba, Aurora McNatt, Lukas Perez;

Sofia Perez, Reagan Cruz, Solveig Hodson, P.K. Iverson;

Robert Yohe IV, Aubrey Phillips, Juniper Keeble.

Made in the USA
Coppell, TX
23 February 2026

72214364R00066